50 Paleo Diet Gulten Free Recipes For Your Sl

The Paleo diet followers say that our current lifestyle and bad eating habits are what make us fat and unhealthy. The basis of this diet is what our ancestors, the cavemen ate before agriculture was founded and grains were introduced into the diet. Paleo allows you to eat pretty much whatever you want if it could have been eaten by cavemen (gathers)

We all know processed foods and sugar are not healthy. The PaleoDiet also calls for the eliminate of all grains and legumes. Grains are carbohydrates which turn into sugar when processed by the body, if not used up immediately they turn to fat. Gluten is a protein found in grains such as wheat, rye, barley. Much of our population is now being diagnosed as gluten intolerant; causing health issues such as: dermatitis, joint aches, acid reflux, and even reproductive issues. Lectins are natural toxins found in grains; our gastrointestinal tract reacts to lectins. Lectins interfere with the natural ability to repair normal wear to the intestinal tract, causing severe damages. Sugar of course inhibits weight loss and a healthy lifestyle. Sugar creates an energy spike then crash. And yet again if the energy is not used up immediately it turns to fat.

Paleo diet eliminates grains, legumes, sugar, starches and processed foods. So what can you eat? Healthy fats, fresh caughtseafood (farmed fish has high mercury levels), lean meats (grass not grain fed), vegetables, fruits, nuts & seeds. Dairy is questionable; if you love milk try a substitute of almond or coconut. Store purchased dairy milk offers no nutritional benefits because when it is put through the homogenization process it 'locks' in all the calcium and vitamins so that our bodies cannot absorb them . Almond and coconut milks are lower in fat & calories, and have higher levels of calcium and vitamins.

By now you are either doing the Paleo or you are thinking of started it. If you have decided to try the Paleo diet, or you are already on it I am going to offer you 50 slow cooker/Crockpot recipes that follow the Paleo lifestyle.

As the author of this book I would just like to say that at the time of this writing, I have been on The Paleo Diet for 6 weeks and have already lost 21 pounds and feel great. Use the recipes and I am sure you will get the same results!

Categories':

- **Beef**

- **Chicken & Turkey**

- **Pork**

- **Soups & Misc.**

Beef Stew

2 T. coconut oil

Large onion

2 T. chili powder

2 t. sea salt

1 t. cumin

1 t. garlic

2 pounds beef stew meat

4 diced tomatoes

2 diced green chilies

1-2 diced jalapenos

½ t. oregano

½ t. thyme

1 bay leaf

Sliced mushrooms

2 carrots chopped

2 zucchini chopped

1 red pepper chopped

5 kale leaves chopped

Cilantro & green onions as garnish

Cold thicken coconut milk

Melt coconut oil in skillet, brown onions and garlic (if using fresh). Mix chili powder, salt, cumin, and garlic if not using fresh, roll meat in mixture, add to pan and brown on all sides.

Place all ingredients except garnishes and coconut milk, into crock-pot/slow cooker, add 3 cups water or beef broth. Cook on high about 4 hours, medium about 6 hours, low about 8 hours; until meat is cooked through. Garnish to taste, add spoon of thick coconut milk to top.

Beef n Broccoli

Coconut oil

2 garlic cloves, smashed

1 pound sirloin cut thin

2T lemon juice

1T flax meal

2t ginger

2 t dried red pepper

2t black pepper

½ c broth

2 c broccoli, chopped

2 c carrots, chopped

Green onion, chopped

Brown beef in coconut oil with salt, add to slow cooker with rest of ingredients. Cook until beef is cooked through and veggies are to your desired softness. High about 3-4 hours.

Stroganoff

1 pound beef chunked

6 T. butter or coconut oil

Onion

8 oz mushrooms

2 cloves garlic smashed

½ c dry white wine

1 c beef broth

1 c coconut milk

1 T parsley

Salt and pepper

Brown onions, garlic and beef in coconut oil or butter, can also sauté mushrooms with this if you like. When beef is browned well on all sides, add to slow cooker. Pour wine into pan and stir to loosen bits stuck on bottom. Pour in milk and broth, stir until saucy. Add to slow cooker along with rest of ingredients. Cook high about 3-4 hours until meat is fully cooked. Serve over spaghetti squash or zucchini noodles.

Beef Mushroom Stew

5 lb beef
4 cloves garlic, smashed
1 onion, chopped
2 carrots, chopped
2 celery stalks chopped
8 ounces mushrooms

2 c broth
1 can diced/crushed tomatoes (or 3fresh)
1/3 cup balsamic vinegar
1 orange
2 stalks rosemary
 Salt & pepper

Brown meat in coconut oil with garlic, onion, celery: until browned on all sides. Add everything to slow cooker. Cook until meat is tender. About 3-4 hours on high.

Meatballs — good

1 lb ground meat
1 lb sausage
1/2 c onion-chopped
1/4 c almond flour
1 egg
1 T Italian seasoning
1 T basil
1 T garlic, smashed
salt & pepper to taste
28 oz. organic tomatoes

Combine all but tomatoes. Shape into balls. Olive oil slow cooker, place meatballs in, pour tomatoes on top. Cook high 4 hours, low 6 hours

Spaghetti Sauce

2 lbs browned ground sirloin or turkey
3 Cups tomato sauce or juice

1 c beef stock
Salt & pepper
½ t red pepper
1 onion chopped
2 small zucchini
2 small yellow squash
Large can crushed tomatoes
5-6 garlic cloves smashed
2 bell peppers chopped

Place all in Crockpot, let cook on low all day. Serve over spaghetti squash.

Rubbed Roast

2 T coffee grounds
½ t. ground chipotle
1 t. cocoa
¼ t. cinnamon
½ Garlic powder
1 T oregano
1 T cumin
1 t salt
Mix ingredients together and set aside.

½ T. coconut oil
2.5 lb roast
¾ c broth

Melt coconut oil in frying pan, med/high. Roll and press spice mix all over the roast. Use all of it, press and rub it in really well. Carefully place in hot pan to sear until all sides have a nice crust. Put in onions in slow cooker, place roast on top, pour broth over top. 5 hours on high, 7 hours on low, until meat is tender and cooked through.

Ginger Flank Steak

3 inches of ginger root-grated

¼ c tamari

Zest & juice of 2 limes

Salt & pepper

2 lbs flank steak

Oil Crockpot, lay meat in bottom, mix rest of ingredients and pour over. Cook low 6-8 hours.

Indian Spice Beef

4 6oz portions of beef sirloin
1 T. cumin
1 T. coriander
1 t. turmeric
1 t. allspice
1 t. smoked paprika
1 T. grill seasoning
½ cup broth

Mix spices, rub steak with olive oil, then with rub mix. Oil Crockpot, place in bottom.

Add broth. Cook low 6-8 hours.

Veal Chops with Marsala Fig Sauce

4 thick bone-in veal
4 t. grill seasoning
2 t. fennel
2 t. coriander
16 dried figs
2/3 c Marsala wine
4-5 sprigs of thyme
Salt & pepper to taste

Mix grill season, fennel and coriander; rub chops, place in oiled slow cooker. Mix rest of ingredients and pour over. Cook low 6-8 hours.

Red Wine Roast

1 4lbs roast;
½ c butter or coconut oil
3 T. Worcestershire sauce
3 cloves garlic, smashed
3 sprig thyme
¾ cup red wine;
Sea salt and freshly ground black pepper to taste;

Melt oil in large frying pan, sear roast. Place in slow cooker with rest of ingredients and cooking fat and juice from frying pan. Cook 4 hours on high until meat is tender. This can be roasted in the oven too for an hour at 350.

Beef & Cabbage

okay, shred cabbage, use less regular Paprika (maybe omit it)

1 head cabbage-washed & separated
3/4 lb ground beef
3/4 lb ground pork
1 t onion flakes
2 t minced garlic
1 T paprika
3 t. Smoked paprika
1/4 t. cinnamon
Salt & pepper
1 can crushed tomatoes
2 T coconut sugar

Brown meats, add sauce ingredients to skillet. In Crockpot, add a bit of water in the

bottom, layer cabbage and meat mix. High for 2-3 hours until cabbage soft. It may have a

lot of liquid, let rest out of Crockpot for 20-30 minutes.

Cheeseburger-Meatloaf

2.5 lbs ground beef-lean
2 whole eggs
1 t. ground black pepper
1 t. sea salt
1/2 t. smoked paprika
2 t. onion powder
4 oz sharp cheddar cheese

Large handful of chard or kale leaves
1 onion
2 jalapenos
 Dill pickle slices

Mix meat, salt, pepper, onion, paprika, eggs; divide into 3

Rub oil in Crockpot, press 1/3 meat mix into bottom leave a bit of room around edge.

Add cheese leaves, onion, pickles, jalapenos, and any other toppings you like: bacon,

avocado, etc. Take second 1/3 of meat and flatten out place on top, seal sides together

with bottom layer so toppings stay in. Repeat for next layer. You can add different

toppings to different layers. Run hands down sides between meat and cooker, make sure

nothing is hanging out. Top with tomato sauce or ketchup-optional. I do not like tomato

based sauces, so I wait until I serve it. Cook 2 ½ hrs high, 5 hrs low.

Beef & Cauliflower

Beef roast large enough for your family

2 heads of cauliflower (we love this stuff!)

Garlic

Onion

Salt & pepper to taste

Cheese (if you are a dairy Paleo)

You can do this two ways. If you have a multi Crockpot you can do the roast and cauliflower separate and mashed it. Place meat and cauliflower in Crockpot(s) with a bit of broth, spices. Cook high 5-6 hours until very tender.

You can put it all in one large Crockpot and mash the cauliflower after or not. If you are not mashing the cauliflower you can omit the cheese altogether. I mash mine with cheese, garlic, salt & pepper. To mash cauliflower I use a stick blender, it gets really creamy that way.

Yam Casserole

2 lbs ground beef

½ lb bacon

8 eggs

3-4 lg yams

1 white onion

1 red onion

Garlic, salt, pepper, cayenne, paprika, oregano

Peel and slice yams. Chop bacon and brown in skillet. Drain on plate. Brown ground beef with onions, garlic and other spices to taste. Beat eggs, add other spices if desired.

Oil Crockpot, layer yams, beef, bacon in crock after layers are in, pour in eggs. Cook low 5-6 hours. Can eat right away or chill and slice.

Lemon-Garlic-Herb Chicken with prosciutto wrapped asparagus

5 cloves garlic-smashed
Salt
1/3 c olive oil
2 lemons
1 t. fennel seed
5 sprigs rosemary
Parsley
4 boneless breasts
4 boneless thighs
1 lb asparagus
8 slices prosciutto
1 c fresh basil
½ cut fresh mint
3-4 T pine nuts

Place chicken in Crockpot; take garlic, basil, mint, nuts, salt & pepper blend in food processor turn on, stream in ¼-1/3 cup olive oil until a thick sauce forms. Pour over chicken. Take asparagus in four bundles wrap with 2 slices prosciutto, place on top of chicken. Pout remainder of sauce over. Cook Low 6-8 hours until chicken is cooked through. If you have a small Crockpot you might only use half the chicken.

French White Burgundy Chicken

1 T. olive oil
4 slices bacon
½ almond flour
2 lbs chicken tenders
Salt & pepper to taste
½ lb mushrooms
3 celery stalks chopped
1 carrot chopped
2 parsnips peeled & chopped
2 T. fresh thyme chopped
4 T. coconut oil
2 c French White Burgundy wine
1 c chicken stock
2 c pearl onions

Chop bacon and brown in skillet with olive oil, brown chicken. Place in Crockpot with

veggies; mix rest of ingredients pour over chicken and veggies. Cook low 4-6 hours.

Chorizo & Chicken Chili

2 lbs diced chicken
½ lb Spanish chorizo medium size pieces
2 onions chopped
4 garlic cloves- smashed
Pepper
1 T smoked paprika
1 T cumin
½ c dry sherry or Rioja
2 c vegetable juice

2-3 c chicken broth
Parsley
5-6 piquillo peppers or 4 roasted red bell peppers
Hot sauce
½ c slivered almonds

Add chicken & veggies into slow cooker, mix rest of ingredients but almonds. Cook low

6-8 hours until chicken fully cooked, garnish with almonds.

Chicken Garlic Sheppard's Pie

2-3 lbs sweet potatoes cut up
1 T olive oil
2 lbs chicken breasts- diced
Black pepper
1 c carrots chopped
1 c peas
1 bunch scallions- sliced
2 T almond flour
½ c white wine
1 ½ c chicken stock
1 T Dijon mustard
6 sprigs tarragon
2 egg yolks
¼ c fresh parsley
¼ almond or coconut milk

Oil Crockpot, add chicken veggies, and season. Mix liquids together, beat in egg yolks and flour until smooth, pour over chicken and veggies.

Bacon Wrapped Chicken with Pecans

4 boneless breasts
Salt & pepper to taste
½ c pecans
2 scallions sliced
4 slices of bacon
2 T. almond flour
1 c broth
½ coconut milk
2 T grainy mustard

Butterfly cut the breasts, salt & pepper, sprinkle with scallions and pecans, roll breasts wrap with bacon. You can put a long toothpick through to keep them closed. Lay in Crockpot, mix liquid and beat in flour, pour over chicken. Cook low 6-7 hours until chicken is fully cooked.

Mango-Pineapple Chicken

3-5 lbs chicken, I like boneless 'wings' strips of breasts are great!
1 T. coconut oil

1 mango
16 oz crushed pineapple in natural juice
2 jalapenos
1 habanera
4 garlic cloves
6 oz tomato paste
1 c beef broth
1 T ACV
2 t. paprika
2 t. cayenne
½ c coconut milk

Melt oil in skillet on medium, add chilies and garlic about 5 minutes, add fruit for another 10 minutes, add broth, ACV, tomato paste, spices. Let simmer, covered about 60 minutes.

Blend with stick blender.

Place chicken in oiled slow cooker, pour sauce over & stir. Cook low 5-6 hours.

Artichoke Chicken

1 ½ lb chicken breasts
6 oz roasted red peppers
15 oz Artichoke Hearts
2 t. Worcestershire
10 oz coconut milk
Salt & pepper to taste
2 c shredded cheese (if you use dairy)
If you don't use dairy, you can add ½ c almond flour to thicken

Put everything in Crockpot on low for 6-8 hours.

Apricot Chicken

½ c no sugar apricot preserves
2 T. dried onion or chop 1 small onion
6 chicken breasts-frozen

Place chicken in slow cooker, mix onion and preserves pour over chicken. Cook on low

5-6 hours.

Chicken & Shrimp

2 lbs boneless skinless chicken
1 onion- chopped
2 T. coconut oil
2 garlic cloves-smashed
¼ c parsley
½ c white wine
12 oz tomato sauce
1 t. basil
1 lb uncooked shrimp

Melt oil in skillet; add onion & garlic, brown chicken. Place in Crockpot with remainder of ingredients, except shrimp. Cook low 4-5 hours. Stir in shrimp cook 30-45 minutes on high, or 90 minutes on low.

Cranberry Chicken

2 lbs boneless, skinless chicken
½ c onion-chopped
2 t. coconut oil
½ t. cinnamon
¼ t. ginger
1/8 t. nutmeg
1/8 t. allspice
1 c orange juice
2 t. grated orange peel

2 c cranberries
Salt to taste

Brown chicken in coconut oil, add salt to taste. Add everything to Crockpot; cook low 6-7 hours. To thicken sauce ad ¼-1/2 cup coconut or almond flour.

Paprika Chicken

4 boneless breasts
2 lbs sweet potatoes
2 carrots
1 onion
1 t. parsley
1 t. salt
¼ t. pepper
4 T. coconut oil
2 T. smoke paprika
1 T. lemon juice
1 t. Worcestershire
1 T. honey
¼ t. cumin

Cut potatoes, carrots and onion into chunks add to Crockpot with parsley, salt, pepper

and 2 T. oil. Mix 2 T. oil with paprika lemon juice, Worcestershire, honey and cumin, rub

chicken with mix lay on top of veggies. Cook low 7-9 hours.

Sweet N Sour Chicken

4 T. coconut oil
¾ c tomato sauce
½ c white vinegar
3 T. Worcestershire
2 garlic cloves-smashed
Salt & pepper to taste
Red pepper or cayenne

1 ½ c broth
6 boneless breasts
8 oz pineapple-crushed

Place chicken in Crockpot, mix oil, tomato paste, vinegar, Worcestershire, garlic, salt, peppers, broth; pour over chicken. Cook low 5-7 hours, add pineapple and cook 20 more minutes.

Almond Chicken

4-6 chicken breasts
12 oz coconut milk
1 T. lemon juice
1/3 c mayonnaise
½ celery
¼ onion
¼ pimiento
½ c almonds
Parsley

Place chicken in Crockpot, milk, lemon juice, mayo, celery, onions, pimiento; pour over chicken. Cook 5-7 hours. Garnish with almonds and parsley.

Chicken-Lime Cilantro

1 whole chicken
Black pepper, sea salt (t. each) chili powder, cayenne powder, ground cumin1 T. each)
1/2 c lime juice
1 whole lime for stuffing
2 bunches cilantro.
3 garlic cloves- smashed
1 T. olive oil.

Wash your chicken. Coat with dry rub.

Combine your lime juice, cilantro, garlic, and olive oil in blender until even.

Poke holes in the whole lime. Sprinkle with chili powder, stuff inside chicken.

Place chicken in large Ziploc, pour in wet ingredients. Seal, leave overnight in refrigerator.

Put chicken in slow cooker plus any marinade from bag.

Low for 6 to 8 hours.

Coconut Mango Chicken

1 lb chicken
Can coconut milk
2 mangos
Dried chipotle flaked

Pour milk into Crockpot, chunk mango add to milk, cut chicken bite size, add then chipotle, mix. 3 hrs on high, 5 hours low.

Coconut Chicken

Chicken to feed your crew
Lemongrass
4 garlic cloves
Ginger
1 c coconut milk
2 T. fish sauce
3 T. coconut flakes

1 onion

Salt & pepper to taste, any other spices you like.

Place onion in Crockpot, place chicken on top. Blend rest of ingredients into sauce and

pour over, stir. On LOW 4-5 hours.

Chicken & Yams

3 yams
4 chicken breasts
4 shallots
2 T. rosemary
Garlic, salt, pepper to taste
1 c broth

Peel and cut yams into bite size pieces. Oil Crockpot; add yams and spices, chicken. Stir

to coat. Cook low 5-6 hours, until chicken is done through.

Chicken & Dumplings

2 lbs Chicken breasts or thigh fillets
2 c broth
2 Yams
4 carrots
3-4 celery stalks
1 onion
4 mushrooms
Garlic
Salt & pepper to taste
2-3 T coconut or almond flour

Wash, cut everything in bite size chunks. Put all in Crockpot. Cook low 4-5 hours. When veggies are tender and chicken is cooked through, add flour to a very small amount of water or cold broth, stir well, pour into crock and stir well to thicken broth. Cover and turn on high while you mix up dumplings.

4 lg eggs, ¼ c butter, ¼ t. baking powder, ¼ t. salt, 1/3 c coconut flour: mix well drop by teaspoon on top of meat and veggies. Cover leave on high until dumplings are cooked. 20-30 minutes.

Pork

Grape Stuffed Balsamic Sausage Meatballs

2 lbs ground pork
2 t. fennel seeds
Salt & pepper
1 t. crushed red pepper
1 clove garlic- smashed
3 T. Balsamic vinegar
12 red or black seedless grapes
2 c arugula chopped
1 c fresh basil
1 c fresh parsley
Juice of ½ lemon

Mix meat, fennel, salt, pepper, red pepper, garlic, vinegar. Take a grape and stuff into a ball of meat, roll it around to form ball with grape inside. Oil Crockpot, lay meatballs in bottom. Mix rest of ingredients and pour over. Cook low 4-6 hours. Check they are done through.

Apple-Mustard Pork Shoulder

2 lg onions
1 boneless shoulder
Salt & pepper to taste
12 oz apple jelly-no sugar
½ broth
2 T. mustard

Put onions in bottom of Crockpot, place roast on top. Mix remaining ingredients, pour over met. Cook low 6-8 hours, high 2-3 hours.

Salsa Porkchops

4 pork chops
1/2 t.cumin
1/2 t. garlic powder
1/2 t. salt or Mrs. Dash
1/2 t. black pepper
1 T olive oil
1 cup salsa
2 T lime juice

Mix spices, rub chops, sear in hot frying pan with oil. Oil Crockpot, place chops in and pour salsa with lime juice over. Cook 2-3 hours on high.

Stuffed & Wrapped Pork Loin

3-5 lb pork loin

1 lb bacon

Guacamole

3-5 Garlic cloves-smashed & chopped

Salt, pepper, red pepper flakes, cumin, chili powder

Carefully fillet loin in a circular cut. What you are looking for is to "unroll" it, stuff it, and roll it back up. Or alternatively, cut through center almost all the way through. Mix dry spices and rub inside, spread guacamole and sprinkle ¾ of garlic on guacamole, roll or close, rub rest of dry spices and garlic on outside of loin, wrap with bacon as tight as possible, if you have cooking twine tie it up for ease to get out of Crockpot. Oil Crockpot, place loin in crock put a little water or broth in bottom. Cook high 3-4 hours, low 6-7. If you tied it up, remove from Crockpot to serving plate, remove twine and slice. If you did not tie up, very carefully remove whole. Slide two spatulas under and lift gently.

Pork & Sauerkraut

3-4 lbs pork
1 lb Sauerkraut
1 C broth
Salt & pepper to taste
3 Garlic cloves-smashed

Melt olive or coconut oil in skillet, rub pork with salt and pepper, and add garlic to skillet. Sear pork on all sides. Place in oiled Crockpot with sauerkraut; add salt & pepper to taste for kraut. Cook high 3-4 hours, low 6-7 hours, until meat is cooked through.

Blackberry Pork

4 oz blackberries

2-3 lb pork loin

A head of broccoli

1 onion

Stock

Olive or coconut oil

1 T balsamic vinegar

Salt & pepper to taste

If you have time to marinade the loin, put vinegar olive oil, salt & pepper together in a plastic bag, rub/smash a few berries onto loin, put in bag and chill overnight.

Oil slow cooker, place loin in, pour marinade over, and add chopped broccoli and rest of berries. Cook high 3-4 hours, low 5-6 hours until pork cooked through. Add feta to broccoli on plate.

Green Chili Pork

2 lbs pork cut up
Coconut or olive oil
1 onion
4 Garlic cloves
 1 t. Oregano
½ t. cumin
3-4 tomatoes
Green chilies (fresh or canned)
2 T. Lime juice

Brown pork in skillet, with onion, garlic, spices. Add to Crockpot with rest of

ingredients. Cook low 4-6 hours.

BBQ Pork

3 lb pork loin
2 T. Tomato paste
½ c ketchup
¼ c Apple Cider Vinegar
¼ c mustard
2 t. tobasco
1 ½ T. Worcestershire
½ t. liquid smoke

Oil slow cooker, place pork in, mix together rest of ingredients, pour over. Cook low 7-8 hours.
Shred pork or slice.

Pork Stuffed Bell Peppers

4 bell peppers
2 lbs ground pork, or pork sausage
½ head cauliflower-riced
8 oz tomato paste
1 onion
4 garlic cloves
1 T. Italian seasoning

Cut tops off peppers, clean out seeds. Mix rest of ingredients, stuff peppers, place in

Crockpot, add enough water to just cover bottom of crock. Low setting 6 hours.

Crockpot Ham

1 Bone-in Ham Shank

1 c Orange Juice

1 t. Orange Zest

1 t. Cloves

3-4 T. Honey if you use it

Oil Crockpot, place ham in bottom, mix juice and spices pour over, drizzle honey over.

Cook low 8-10 hours depending on large your ham is. Baste if you want every couple

hours. This is an amazing way to cook ham, you do not have to be home, and it comes

out fall off the bone tender and juicy!

Spiced Pork Roast

2 lbs Tip pork roast
2 c orange juice
1 c cranberries
¼ coconut flakes or crystals
1 T. coconut vinegar
5 Arbol chilies
1 t. allspice
½ t cloves
½ t ginger
¼ t cayenne
½ adobo season
Salt
Coconut

Mix dry spices, rub roast. Oil Crockpot, place roast in, mix liquids & cranberries pour

over. Cook low 8-10 hours.

Soups & Misc.

Chorizo-Kale

1 lb chorizo
1/2 T coconut oil.
1 can coconut milk.

2 c broth-chicken or beef
1 c water
1 onion-white
1 onion-red
1 jalapeno
Handful of kale
1/4 t. salt.
1/4 t. red pepper or chipotle flakes

Brown chorizo, add everything to Crockpot cook until meat is cooked and onions soft. High 3-4 hours.

Chicken Vegetable Soup

3 lbs cut up chicken- or if you roasted a whole one use the leftovers-save carcass for broth
6-8 c broth
3 sweet potatoes
3 carrots
4 celery stalks
1-2 onions
4-5 cloves garlic
1 c mushrooms
Salt & pepper
2 T. Lemon zest
1 bunch cilantro for garnish-chopped

Throw everything in slow cooker except cilantro. Cook high 2-4 hours, low 6-8 hours. The longer the better flavors! Add cilantro in the bowls.

Squash Soup

Large butternut squash- cut up (peeled)

14 oz coconut milk

2 c chicken broth

1 apple cored

2 carrots- cut up

Place all in slow cooker 4-6 hours low, 3 high; until tender. Use stick blender to mix.

Optional additions to taste: cinnamon, nutmeg, apple cider in place of broth, red curry paste, ginger & curry, jalapeno, bacon, paprika. Can add to soup while cooking or garnish with anything.

Sweet Potato Soup

6 c cut up sweet potatoes
14 oz jar roasted red peppers
14 oz coconut milk
1 c chicken broth
1 onion
2 cloves garlic
½ t crushed red peppers
Salt & pepper to taste

Place all ingredients into Crockpot cook medium 5-6 hours until soft, blend in crock with stick blender, or food processor.

Lamb Meatloaf with Tangy Red Onion & Fire Roasted Tomato Sauce

3 c chicken broth
1 ½ lb ground lamb
Salt & pepper
½- 1 c almond flour
1 egg
1 large garlic cloves, smashed
Olive oil
1 red onion, chopped
2 T balsamic vinegar
28 oz fire-roasted tomatoes

Mix meat, 1/3 c broth, salt, pepper, egg & garlic; mix together to form loaf. Oil Crockpot, press into bottom. Mix rest of ingredients pour over meatloaf. Slide spatula around edges to leave a bit of room for liquids. Cook low 5-7 hours, until cooked through.

Trash Stew

This is when I have leftovers that I cannot make something new out of....
Leftover meat
Leftover veggies
2-4 cups tomato sauce
1-2 c broth
Salt and pepper to taste
Throw it all in Crockpot, cook high 2-4 hours, low 4-5 hours.

CPSIA information can be obtained at www.ICGtesting.com
Printed in the USA
BVOW05s0149210813

329159BV00001B/4/P

9 781484 869185